POET, PILGRIM, REBEL

The Story of Anne Bradstreet, America's First Published Poet

by Katie Munday Williams

illustrated by Tania Rex

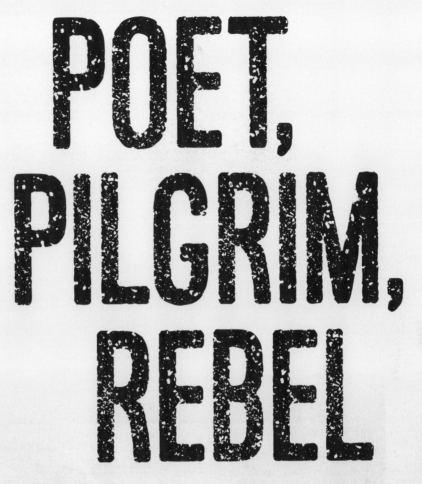

beaming books
MINNEAPOLIS

England
1620

Eight-year-old Anne Dudley was different from other girls. She had a secret. She wanted to be a writer. But girls weren't allowed to attend school, and they certainly weren't allowed to be writers.

Like other Puritan girls, Anne learned how to read and write at home so she could study the Bible. She also learned to obey her parents and to cook and keep house.

Most days, Anne rushed through her chores, then snuck
to the library, her favorite room in the house. There,
her father shared his love of poetry. Anne devoured
books like corn pudding.

Some nights, Anne listened to her father's friends discuss music, astronomy, and medicine. Anne was encouraged to voice her opinions, something girls were not usually allowed to do.

Listen and learn. Listen and learn. This was the rhythm of Anne's days.

Anne and her father read poetry together and studied how poems worked. The words comforted her. She turned to poems when she felt worried or sad.

When Anne was sixteen, she married her father's assistant, Simon Bradstreet. Simon was kind and quick to laugh. Anne loved discussing her thoughts and opinions with him.

Together, they admired astronomers, marveled over musicians, and pored over poetry.

The year Anne turned eighteen, everything changed. The king of England disagreed with the Puritans on how to worship God. He ordered Puritan churches to be closed or burned.

Ten years before, a small group of Puritans had decided to move to what they called the New World, an ocean away. Now Anne's husband and father decided their families would go too.

Anne cried in secret about leaving her home. But she did not complain. She tucked her thoughts into her bonnet and prepared for the long voyage.

The trip across the ocean was difficult. The ship bucked and creaked. Passengers were crammed together. Anne was sad and bored. With no room to spare on the ship, her books had to be left behind.

In Massachusetts, they joined a struggling colony of about two hundred people. The Puritans had claimed land where Indigenous people known as Algonquians lived. Many Puritans were sick from lack of food and medicine.

Anne and her family set to work caring for the sick and building the Puritan community they had dreamed of.

Work and sleep. Work and sleep. Anne's life had a new rhythm.

Even in this new home, Anne
found poetry all around her.
Bang, bang, bang!
Hammers reminded Anne
of the rhythm of poems.

Chirrup, chirrup! The song of the birds cheered her as she worked.

It was a hard life. Anne worried about the colony and her family, but as a good Puritan woman, she kept quiet.

When Anne was twenty, she became very sick. She coughed and shivered in her bed. Anne worried that she was being punished for her doubts about the New World.

When she finally got better, Anne wanted to do something to show how thankful she was.

Anne again turned to poetry for comfort. This time, she wrote her own poem.

Anne knew that outspoken women could be banished from the colony. She also knew the Puritans valued religious poetry. So Anne made her first poem about thanking God. She praised God for healing her, and she promised to be a good person.

Paper was as precious as food. Anne couldn't waste a single piece.

Line by line, she had first written her poem in her mind.

When it felt finished, Anne shaped the words with her pen.

Proudly, and with a little fear, Anne shared her poem.
She showed it to her husband, her mother and
sisters, and her minister.

To her delight, nobody told her to stop writing. Instead, everyone praised her poem. From then on, words flowed from her quill.

The following year, Anne had even more reason to feel blessed. She gave birth to her first child.

Simon was often away for work, and Anne
found herself alone most nights. At first,
she was sad and missed him terribly. Then she
realized that this time to herself was an opportunity.

At night, while the baby slept, Anne lit a candle
and sat with her books and parchment.
All the thoughts she had kept
to herself over the years tumbled
out onto the paper.

The colony grew, and so did Anne's family. Anne had seven more children. She also boldly branched out in her writing. Anne wrote about her feelings, her family, and her opinions on world politics.

It was unheard of for a woman to write this way! Anne wanted a way to stay respectable while also writing the way she wanted to. She decided to humbly make fun of her own poems. She wrote about what she called her "feeble" attempts at writing.

It worked. Men saw that here was a woman who wrote well,
and who was also a great wife and mother.

One day, Anne's brother-in-law took Anne's poems with him to England. Anne hoped they would calm growing tensions between England and the colonies. Many of the poems begged for peace.

Months went by as Anne waited anxiously for news. Would people accuse her of copying from a man? She feared she would be cast out if men disapproved of her writing.

Almost three years later, in 1650, a book of her poems was published. When Anne learned about it months later, she was already famous.

Anne's rebellious writing was no longer a secret. Her beautiful, clever poetry was beloved on both sides of the Atlantic Ocean. She received many letters thanking her for her writing.

Anne had shown that women could be great writers. She had paved the way for others. And she was proud of her message of peace, harmony, and love.

hove you fore
my dear hovi

AUTHOR'S NOTE

Anne's life as a dutiful Puritan continued. She lovingly raised her large family and remained a model member of her community. As her children grew up and had families of their own, Anne found more time for her writing. She updated her first book and wrote many more poems. Anne even developed her very own kind of poetic rhythm.

Anne Dudley Bradstreet is my great-grandmother x 14. Born more than four hundred years ago on March 20, 1612, Anne was spirited and ambitious. Anne's mother made it her mission to "cure" Anne of these unladylike traits. Anne learned how to keep her innermost thoughts to herself while continuing to do what she loved most—read and write.

Anne's accomplishments are incredible for any writer of her time but are especially so for a woman. She wrote more than six thousand lines of poetry during a period of great upheaval in her life and her world. She was pregnant or nursing for most of that time, her husband was often gone on business, and England and the thirteen American colonies were often fighting.

It's important to note that many Indigenous people, the Algonquian tribes, were already living on the land that Puritans and other colonists claimed. Many, many Algonquians were killed by war and diseases brought by the colonists. The Algonquians tried to share the land with colonists through trade and alliances. But over time, the colonists violently forced the Algonquians off the land.

Troubled by the way women were dismissed in her community, Anne wrote extensively about women's rights. She disguised her opinions within the context of her other subjects. She often pretended to criticize her own writing in an effort to downplay her accomplishments in the eyes of men.

There is debate over whether Anne knew that her brother-in-law had taken her poems to England. While most believe she did not, some of us believe otherwise. The last poem in her book gives several clues, and I believe she knew exactly what she was doing when she handed her masterpiece to her brother-in-law.

Anne's diligent research, strict adherence to poetic meter, and not-so-subtle wit showed men and women alike that her creative mind was a force to be reckoned with. Today, Anne Bradstreet is hailed as an early feminist, a free-thinker, and the author of some of the most beautiful, profound poetry ever written.

I am obnoxious to each carping tongue

Who says my hand a needle better fits.

A Poet's Pen all scorn I should thus wrong,

For such despite they cast on female wits.

If what I do prove well, it won't advance.

They'll say it's stol'n, or else it was by chance.

–Anne Bradstreet,
from "Prologue"

TIMELINE

1612—On March 20, Anne Dudley is born to Thomas and Dorothy Dudley in North Hamptonshire, England.

1620—Anne's father gets a job as a steward for the Earl of Lincoln, and Anne's family moves to the earl's house, Sempringham Manor.

1620—The first Puritans, also known as Pilgrims, leave England on the *Mayflower*, seeking religious freedom in the American colonies. The area was already home to many Algonquian people, including the Wampanoag and Pennacook tribes.

1622—Simon Bradstreet begins working for Thomas Dudley; he and Anne develop a close friendship.

1628—Anne and Simon are married.

1630—The Dudley/Bradstreet family sails to America on the ship *Arbella*.

1632—Anne falls ill, and after recovering writes her first poem.

1632—Anne has the first of eight children, a boy named Samuel.

1634—Thomas Dudley is elected governor of Massachusetts Bay Colony.

1638—An outspoken Puritan woman named Anne Hutchinson is banished from Massachusetts Bay Colony for speaking about disagreements with the Puritan church.

1642–1651—The English Civil War is fought.

1650—Anne's book, *The Tenth Muse, Lately Sprung Up in America*, is published in England.

1672—Anne Bradstreet dies on September 16 at the age of sixty.

1678—The first American version of *The Tenth Muse* is published in America with Anne's revisions, along with a new collection of poems.

To Aaron, Rose, and James for encouraging my curiosity,
and to my parents and sisters for always believing in me. —K.M.W.

To my husband and son. —T.R.

Text copyright ©2021 Katie Munday Williams
Illustrations copyright ©2021 Beaming Books

Published in 2021 by Beaming Books, an imprint of 1517 Media.
All rights reserved. No part of this book may be reproduced without
the written permission of the publisher. Email copyright@1517.media.
Printed in the United States of America.

27 26 25 24 23 22 21   1 2 3 4 5 6 7 8

Hardcover ISBN: 978-1-5064-6306-3
Ebook ISBN: 978-1-5064-6887-7

Library of Congress Cataloging-in-Publication Data

Names: Williams, Katie Munday, author. | Rex, Tania, illustrator.
Title: Poet, pilgrim, rebel : the story of Anne Bradstreet, America's first
   published poet / by Katie Munday Williams ; illustrated by Tania Rex.
Description: Minneapolis, MN : Beaming Books, 2021. | Audience: Ages 5-8 |
   Summary: "This charming picture book biography tells the inspiring story
   of Anne Bradstreet, a gifted Puritan writer who overcame barriers to
   become America's first published poet"-- Provided by publisher.
Identifiers: LCCN 2021001972 (print) | LCCN 2021001973 (ebook) | ISBN
   9781506463063 (hardcover) | ISBN 9781506468877 (ebook)
Subjects: LCSH: Bradstreet, Anne, 1612?-1672–Juvenile literature. | Poets,
   American--Colonial period, ca. 1600-1775--Biography--Juvenile
   literature.
Classification: LCC PS712 .W55 2021 (print) | LCC PS712 (ebook) | DDC
   811/.1 [B]--dc23
LC record available at https://lccn.loc.gov/2021001972
LC ebook record available at https://lccn.loc.gov/2021001973

VN004589; 9781506463063; MAY2021

Beaming Books
510 Marquette Avenue
Minneapolis, MN 55402

Beamingbooks.com

1632—Anne has the first of eight children, a boy named Samuel.

1634—Thomas Dudley is elected governor of Massachusetts Bay Colony.

1638—An outspoken Puritan woman named Anne Hutchinson is banished from Massachusetts Bay Colony for speaking about disagreements with the Puritan church.

1642–1651—The English Civil War is fought.

1650—Anne's book, *The Tenth Muse, Lately Sprung Up in America*, is published in England.

1672—Anne Bradstreet dies on September 16 at the age of sixty.

1678—The first American version of *The Tenth Muse* is published in America with Anne's revisions, along with a new collection of poems.

To Aaron, Rose, and James for encouraging my curiosity,
and to my parents and sisters for always believing in me. —K.M.W.

To my husband and son. —T.R.

Text copyright ©2021 Katie Munday Williams
Illustrations copyright ©2021 Beaming Books

Published in 2021 by Beaming Books, an imprint of 1517 Media.
All rights reserved. No part of this book may be reproduced without
the written permission of the publisher. Email copyright@1517.media.
Printed in the United States of America.

27 26 25 24 23 22 21   1 2 3 4 5 6 7 8

Hardcover ISBN: 978-1-5064-6306-3
Ebook ISBN: 978-1-5064-6887-7

Library of Congress Cataloging-in-Publication Data

Names: Williams, Katie Munday, author. | Rex, Tania, illustrator.
Title: Poet, pilgrim, rebel : the story of Anne Bradstreet, America's first
   published poet / by Katie Munday Williams ; illustrated by Tania Rex.
Description: Minneapolis, MN : Beaming Books, 2021. | Audience: Ages 5-8 |
   Summary: "This charming picture book biography tells the inspiring story
   of Anne Bradstreet, a gifted Puritan writer who overcame barriers to
   become America's first published poet"-- Provided by publisher.
Identifiers: LCCN 2021001972 (print) | LCCN 2021001973 (ebook) | ISBN
   9781506463063 (hardcover) | ISBN 9781506468877 (ebook)
Subjects: LCSH: Bradstreet, Anne, 1612?-1672--Juvenile literature. | Poets,
   American--Colonial period, ca. 1600-1775--Biography--Juvenile
   literature.
Classification: LCC PS712 .W55 2021 (print) | LCC PS712 (ebook) | DDC
   811/.1 [B]--dc23
LC record available at https://lccn.loc.gov/2021001972
LC ebook record available at https://lccn.loc.gov/2021001973

VN004589; 9781506463063; MAY2021

Beaming Books
510 Marquette Avenue
Minneapolis, MN 55402

Beamingbooks.com